Wa

2023–2024

Susan H. Swetnam

LITURGICAL PRESS

Collegeville, Minnesota

www.litpress.org

Nihil Obstat: Rev. Robert C. Harren, J.C.L., *Censor Librorum*
Imprimatur: ✠ Most Rev. Donald J. Kettler, J.C.L., D.D., Bishop of
St. Cloud, January 25, 2023

Cover design by Monica Bokinskie.
Cover art courtesy of Getty Images.

ISSN: 1550-803X
ISBN: 978-0-8146-6702-6   978-0-8146-6704-0 (ebook)

Introduction

As 8:00 a.m. Mass began in our Rocky Mountain town on the First Sunday of Advent last year, the world was still dark outside the stained glass windows. Snow-falling-on-snow had made the roads challenging. Nevertheless, the church was filled with bright, warm energy as those present fervently joined us musicians in the gathering hymn: "O Come, O Come, Emmanuel." Voices rose and faces shone as the congregation leaned into that ancient litany of O Antiphons, claiming kinship with centuries of worshippers who have intoned that hymn's hopes, fears, and longings in the year's darkest time.

Christians often say that we're an "Easter people," and certainly that's true—Christ's resurrection, with its promise of salvation, is everything. Yet these winter weeks, too, speak to our situation as people challenged always and everywhere to maintain hope despite the "clouds of night" manifested in our lives as sickness, loneliness, sorrow, and eventually death.

How much this Advent-Christmas time has to teach us about the practice of faith year-round! Advent's waiting trains us in essential patience. The virtues often honored on its four Sundays—hope, love, joy, and peace—echo the eternal future promised to the faithful, while reminding us that even now we can be sharing these gifts with our weary world. The Christmas season reminds us of God's timeless faithfulness, inviting us to relax into the assurance of divine love, to live our faith with resolve as the liturgy replays the marvels of our Savior's earliest days.

It's sad, then, that these weeks are often experienced as speedy, busy, fleeting. For so many, if Advent is recognized at all, it disappears in a blur of restless yearning and frantic attempts to engineer the perfect holiday. The two weeks of Christmas become an afterthought, a time to recuperate.

But you've opened this book, indicating a desire to make space, to focus on the season's Scriptures. Pope Francis has encouraged such daily practice, emphasizing that we should not delay in seeking God, but should seize the present moment as the proper time. The present, after all, is where we live. It is where God finds us.

In that spirit, I hope this book helps you savor every day of this year's Advent-Christmas celebration. I pray it encourages you to claim kinship with all those who have from age to age found such reassurance, such bright joy, in these familiar words of Scripture.

O come, O come, Emmanuel. Slow us down, help us listen. Comfort us, rescue us, set us free.

FIRST WEEK OF ADVENT

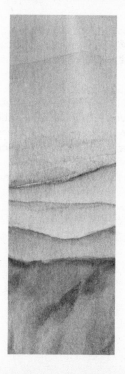

December 3: First Sunday of Advent

The Discipline of Hope

Readings: Isa 63:16b-17, 19b; 64:2-7; 1 Cor 1:3-9;
Mark 13:33-37

Scripture:
[T]he testimony to Christ was confirmed among you, so that
you are not lacking in any spiritual gift as you wait for the
revelation of our Lord Jesus Christ. (1 Cor 1:6-7)

Reflection: Symbolizing hope, the Advent wreath's first
candle invites joyful anticipation, both of the celebration of
Christ's birth and of the host of other joys the Advent and
Christmas seasons offer.

Everyone craves hope, but I'll bet your experience, like
mine, has emphasized how hard hope is to sustain over an
extended period of drought. Paul acknowledged that fact,
reminding the Romans that those who hope by definition
in a state of suspended, trust-based anticipation—a state
vulnerable to the whispers of doubt and distraction. Even
the disciplined St. Teresa of Avila encountered these tempta-
tions. "Watch carefully," she advised her soul, "for everything passes quickly, even though your impatience makes
doubtful what is certain, and turns a very short time into a
long one."

Yet there's a way to keep our hope secure, a discipline
embraced by Paul, Teresa, and legions of ordinary Christians:

while we wait, we can commit to living as though we really, truly believe Jesus' coming is imminent, reforming our hearts *now*, actively seeking him *today*. Our first reading invites us to do just that, encouraging us to identify as people who, despite past transgressions, are eager for God's coming, ready to reconcile, firm in faith.

This year Advent is as short as it can be: just twenty-two days. And so, more than ever, the weeks ahead offer an invitation to practice and maintain resolute hopefulness. What daily rituals of prayer, reading, and charity can you incorporate into this short season, to affirm your faith and hope?

Meditation: Working toward creating something beautiful can help foster patient hope during Advent. One simple option might be to bring dormant narcissus (small, fragrant daffodil) bulbs to winter bloom on a windowsill. (Look for them at garden centers or superstores.) More substantively, revive a dormant friendship by "watering" it with love and bringing it into the sun of ongoing attention.

Prayer: Holy Spirit, may faithful, patient hope inspire my Advent practices this year.

December 4: Monday of the First Week of Advent

Dreaming of Accord among the Nations

Readings: Isa 2:1-5; Matt 8:5-11

Scripture:
They shall beat their swords into plowshares . . .
One nation shall not raise the sword against another,
 nor shall they train for war again. (Isa 2:4)

Reflection: "But won't Ukraine be 'old news' by the time your book is published?" my friend asked. When I told her I'd be reflecting on beating "swords into plowshares," she assumed I'd be alluding to Russia's invasion of Ukraine. "That sounded harsh," she apologized, "but you know what I mean. There will be new wars by then."

She's right. Even if the war in Ukraine rages on, there will be new wars, each conflict's suffering just as raw and timelessly tragic.

One particularly painful aspect of this repetition is its cost to human flourishing. Those who conquer more often than not find that the resources they hoped to exploit have become a devastated mess, incapable of agricultural production or any other yield, potential workers dazed, damaged, resentful.

When will they ever learn? as we used to sing in my idealistic 1960s youth. The cycle of aggressive violence seems unbreakable, soul-shattering in its predictability.

The pairing of today's first reading and Gospel, however, invites us to imagine a different future. Isaiah's idealistic scene offers a dream of accord (and dreaming, it's said, is a first step toward doing). Matthew's story presents a remarkable precedent for détente—for truce—in this world, depicting a military commander who, though a representative of hated Roman occupiers, humbles himself in faith. Nothing is impossible with God, that story demonstrates: not physical healing, not the healing of cultural enmity.

Drawing on Advent's spirit of hope, let us dare to resist our ancient tendency toward tribal warfare. In our words and deeds, let us help ourselves and others imagine what peace might look like.

Meditation: Though ending the sad cycle of national conflicts might be beyond our power, every one of us has the capacity to comfort war's victims. If your community is accepting refugees, consider reaching out personally to newcomers. Befriend a family; ask someone to coffee or lunch; help strangers navigate new places and customs by accompanying them to the grocery store or doctor's office.

Prayer: May I walk in the light of your peace, Loving Savior, modeling it for others.

December 5: Tuesday of the First Week of Advent

Peace among Individuals

Readings: Isa 11:1-10; Luke 10:21-24

Scripture:
The cow and the bear shall be neighbors,
  together their young shall rest . . . (Isa 11:7)

Reflection: Today's Scripture returns to the theme of peace, evoking hope not just for improbable accord between nations but for peace between individual beings.

Isaiah's vision of paradise is especially striking because the "individuals" in question are beasts—creatures we usually imagine as irrational and driven by self-interest—living as if they trusted there were enough resources to go around.

But maybe this isn't so unimaginable after all. Social media videos show puppies and moose dozing together, baby goats and baby lions in joyful communal play, domestic dogs and cats in sweet accord. Even antagonistic members of the same animal species can awe us with their improbable harmony, as happened in my own home recently as my elderly cat was dying. My younger cat, whom the former had always bullied, approached her as she lay trying to remember how to drink from her bowl. Apprehensive about revenge, I moved toward them—and witnessed the younger ever-so-gently and sympathetically touching her nose to her old adversary's.

If they can do it, so can we, right? But our rationality, our long memories for grievances, and the defensive stories we tell ourselves about others seem to interfere.

One exception comes during disasters, when strangers forget differences, comfort each other, work together. Communal trauma, it's been suggested, forces us to rethink our comfortable notions of personal exceptionality, bringing greater awareness of common vulnerability and interests.

Advent Scriptures do the same, reminding us of the longing and hope we all share. As we hear God's voice this season, let us remember this common ground and open our hearts to one another.

Meditation: If you were to follow Isaiah's lead and paint a picture of paradise, who would be the most unlikely human being in your everyday life to rest peacefully by your side? Prayerfully summon common ground; brainstorm what you might you do this Advent to heal the relationship.

Prayer: Loving Father of all living creatures, teach me to live in harmony with my neighbors.

December 6: Wednesday of the First Week of Advent
(Saint Nicholas)

Tending the Flock

Readings: Isa 25:6-10a; Matt 15:29-37

Scripture:
Jesus summoned his disciples and said, "My heart is moved with pity for the crowd . . ." (Matt 15:32)

Reflection: How full of echoes the liturgy is today as its Gospel invites us to marvel at the deeds of Jesus, that greatest of all shepherds, on the feast day of another marvelously generous and selfless pastor, St. Nicholas of Myra.

As you know, the St. Nicholas of history was a very different person than the "St. Nicholas" who appears in "The Night Before Christmas." A fourth-century bishop in Asia Minor renowned for his love for his people, he declined a privileged life to enter God's service. According to legend this servant-leader redeemed poor girls from prostitution, saved hostile sailors' lives by calming a fierce storm, even revived children murdered for food during famine. Many churches have been dedicated him, including four hundred in medieval times alone.

But Nicholas, just like Christ, had both clarity and courage when evil threatened. He's reported to have zealously confronted the heresy of Arius, dramatically torn down pagan temples, and boldly defied authority to accomplish the release of innocent prisoners.

True servants of God, this rounded portrait suggests, understand that both charity and strength are needed at the proper time—as their original mentor Christ did. Neither cloyingly sweet nor constantly inflexible, they're able to adapt, dispensing mercy here, correction there, judging which is appropriate by the lodestar of God's truth.

May the Holy Spirit inspire those who teach and mentor today's seminarians and priests, religious educators and ministers, and all those who lead and influence in our church, that they may raise up future shepherds in this mold.

Meditation: Do you know a priest, deacon, teacher, or minister of any kind whose service lovingly and justly blends generosity and rigor, compassion and direction? Write a note of admiration today, in Nicholas's honor, to such a good shepherd in your life.

Prayer: God of mercy and might, help me be flexible and discerning when I'm called to shepherd others.

Persisting despite Storms

Readings: Isa 26:1-6; Matt 7:21, 24-27

Scripture:
"The rain fell, the floods came, and the winds blew and buf-
feted the house. But it did not collapse . . ." (Matt 7:25)

Reflection: I recently stood outside a neat, modest, rural
house after a hospice massage session, visiting with the
mother of a ten-year-old girl who is dying of brain cancer.
Thanks be to God, the treatment I offered had seemed to
offer at least temporary comfort and pain relief. Relaxed and
smiling, young Emmy had passed my touch on to the kitten
in her lap, petting her pet's leg while I massaged her arm,
its head when I caressed hers, both of them drifting to peaceful sleep.

While you might expect a parent in such a situation to turn
desperate, Emmy's mother was turning to God. "We can't
imagine why this happened, and honestly, we do get mad
at God sometimes," she confessed. "But Brent and I, and
even the other kids, keep telling ourselves that we just have
to believe right now. Faith's all we have."

Why such trials come to good people is an ancient, un-
answerable question. Divine ways are mysterious, indeed.

Matthew's Gospel offers a life-sustaining perspective
when troubles invite us to doubt God's faithfulness—

whether catastrophes like the one confronting Emmy's family, or more minor disruptions of our treasured plans. And come they will, as the wear and tear of mortality and change sooner or later assail houses built on rock foundations *and* those sited on sand.

What Scripture promises isn't a carefree life but the deeper, longer-term assurance that faith will help us persist through such trials to ultimately delight in Christ's presence, when all suffering will be past.

Nobody said that "waiting in joyful hope" was going to be easy. As difficult as it might sometimes be to cultivate trust in a joyful heavenly future, however, we must persist. After all, that discipline isn't just a part of our Christian duty—it might also become the life raft that keeps us, like that little family, from foundering in despair in the here and now.

Meditation: Are life's difficulties distracting you from joyful preparation this Advent? Tell God how you feel, frankly sharing your frustrations, fears, and anger. Pray that you may be renewed and sustained in hope.

Prayer: When trials come, O Lord, may I rest on a firm foundation of trust in you.

December 8:
The Immaculate Conception of the Blessed Virgin Mary

Accepting the Work Designed for Us

Readings: Gen 3:9-15, 20; Eph 1:3-6, 11-12; Luke 1:26-38

Scripture:
Mary said, "Behold, I am the handmaid of the Lord. May it be done to me according to your word." (Luke 1:38)

Reflection: The feast of the Immaculate Conception is a relatively recent celebration, officially dating to Pope Pius IX's decree in 1854. Yet belief in Mary's sinlessness had already been embraced by Catholics. No wonder; surely the woman chosen by God to bear God's son must be exemplary.

Mary certainly demonstrates such transcendent character in today's Gospel story of the annunciation. Though initially stunned by the angel Gabriel's words—which predict a future so astoundingly different from what she must have imagined as a modest, socially obscure young girl—Mary quickly agrees, voicing absolute unity with God's will.

It's a story that inspires awe—and points the way for the rest of us. For we too will face "annunciations" as our lives evolve, occasions when unexpected opportunities, "chance" encounters, failures, losses, and heavenly gifts serve as messengers calling us to paths of service that initially seem incomprehensible and daunting.

Will we sense the Mystery's voice, trusting as Mary did that the One who calls us will sustain us through challenges that seem beyond our capacity? Or will we dismiss the summons out of fear, lack of faith, or stubborn adherence to a status quo we've outgrown?

We can never aspire to Mary's sinlessness, that's for sure. But all of us can hope to echo her obedient words, sure in the truth that, as John Henry Newman wrote, "everyone who breathes" has a specific, God-designed role to play.

Meditation: Spend time throughout the Advent season meditating with an artistic representation of the annunciation: a painting or statue in your church, a piece of artwork reproduced online or in a book. Drink in its inspiration, considering what lessons about humility and pure trust it offers.

Prayer: Give me the grace, Heavenly Father, to accept the callings you send me, however strange they may initially appear.

The Charism of Healing

Readings: Isa 30:19-21, 23-26; Matt 9:35–10:1, 5a, 6-8

Scripture:
[H]e summoned his Twelve Disciples and gave them authority over unclean spirits to drive them out and to cure every disease and every illness. (Matt 10:1)

Reflection: While we no longer use the term "unclean spirits" in relation to human illness, today's Gospel speaks powerfully to our longing for health. If you're experiencing illness or disability, you might imagine yourself among the sick who sought the disciples' healing. If you love someone who's suffering, you'll envy those who could access these Spirit-inspired healers.

Would that such healers walked among us today! But perhaps they do—at least, the experience of some health-care workers I know suggests that heavenly help is still available. "It was like something took over and guided me," a Catholic nurse shared over coffee one day. "When that patient started breathing again, I spontaneously said out loud, without thinking beforehand, 'Thank you, Holy Spirit.'" A mental health counselor similarly confessed, "Sometimes the right question just pops out. Those moments just seem inspired. *Wow, where did that come from?* I ask myself."

You may have witnessed such circumstances outside of medical realms, too, as when unpremeditated words heal conflict in a family or workplace, or when you hear yourself suddenly speak tenderly to calm another's panic, despite your own anxiety. These might be small, modest tastes of inspiration, but they too play a significant role in healing the world.

"Charism" can seem a weighty concept, more at home in the ancient past than the present. Nevertheless, this distinctive charism of healing still reaches us as today's disciples, enveloping us, working through us as the Father's voice and hands.

Meditation: Set aside time for sharing stories of healing or being healed in a faith-based group in your home or parish. Listen for examples of the Holy Spirit's intervention in human action, and give thanks. Let these stories make you more aware of when the Holy Spirit is reaching into your circumstances, seeking your help to salve various wounds.

Prayer: Spirit of God, help me to become one who shares your peace wherever healing is needed.

SECOND WEEK OF ADVENT

Attentive Love

Readings: Isa 40:1-5, 9-11; 2 Pet 3:8-14; Mark 1:1-8

Scripture:
Every valley shall be filled in,
    every mountain and hill shall be made low;
the rugged land shall be made a plain,
    the rough country, a broad valley. (Isa 40:4)

Reflection: What a treat today's liturgy offers, with metaphors and images so timelessly appealing that their echoes grace both Handel's *Messiah* and contemporary Christian hits.

In Isaiah's historical context these metaphors weren't just lovely ideas but carried very specific associations, evoking the rough topography of Judah, stretching in elevation from 1,300 feet below sea level to 3,300 feet above. Travel through that mountainous, arid landscape was hard and dangerous. In the world of Isaiah's hearers, today's Scripture voiced exactly the promises this people would have wanted to hear, those of a Father attentive to their struggles.

Would that the love we offer each other might be so specifically and attentively focused! Too often, in our hurry and self-absorption, we simply mouth affectionate platitudes to one another—*I wish you all the love in the world! I hope you feel better soon!*—without taking the time to see and understand what the other really needs.

Such clichés, even well-meant, can have unintended consequences during December in particular, when many people are struggling, feeling excluded from the general happiness of the season. Careless cheery greetings and wishes that seem not to really see or understand the person who is suffering can spark a painful cycle: *No one wants to listen to my problems. No one imagines or cares what I need.*

As we celebrate love today in the lighting of the Advent wreath's second candle, may we follow our God's example in extending an attentive, personalized gaze.

Meditation: Can you identify people in your parish, at work, or among family and friends who might welcome help this season, either emotional or practical? Try to ascertain what they need most and dedicate yourself to offering it during the season ahead.

Prayer: Loving Father, make me into a person who is always attentive to others' challenges, always willing to smooth their specific paths.

Ready to Be Amazed

Readings: Isa 35:1-10; Luke 5:17-26

Scripture:
Then astonishment seized them all and they glorified God, and, struck with awe, they said, "We have seen incredible things today." (Luke 5:26)

Reflection: Though the word "incredible" is now used to describe anything excellent ("That was an incredible dessert!"), its root lies in the Latin verb *credere*, meaning "to believe." In a strict sense, something incredible transcends the boundaries of what can be rationally explained, as a miracle does.

While some deride miracles as ridiculous projections from superstitious minds, C. S. Lewis argued that they actually make a kind of logical sense in a God-created universe where wonders stretch our capacity for understanding. The incredible, he suggests, is "a retelling in small letters of the very same story which is written across the whole world in letters too large for some of us to see." Miracles, in other words, are an entry point for our limited perspectives, a tool to help our untrained eyes learn to grow comfortable with the divine propensity for working in ways beyond our understanding.

The extraordinary healings recounted in today's Scripture function like that, offering onlookers a glimpse of what is possible with God. In particular, the moment when the men lower their friend through the roof—which I always imagine in an exaggerated "Monty Python" style—catches a fundamental truth: when we begin to understand what God is capable of, we won't be able to contain ourselves.

Yes, it can feel risky to open our minds to possibilities that transcend the world's assumptions about what is possible. Yet if we call ourselves followers of this wonder-working Jesus, we have no choice but to stand ready to be amazed.

Meditation: During this season that celebrates the greatest miracle of all time—the incarnation—bolster your own faith in miracles by keeping company with saints and mystics who have written about marvelous divine intervention in their lives. Set aside time during Advent for exploring the writing of historic mystics like Hildegard of Bingen (1098–1179) or Faustina (1905–1938), or a more recent mystic like Thomas Merton (1915–1968).

Prayer: Open my eyes, Lord. Help me to perceive the light of your face, ever glowing through this world's seemingly workaday surface.

December 12: Our Lady of Guadalupe

Our Lady Loves Our Music

Readings: Zech 2:14-17 or Rev 11:19a; 12:1-6a, 10ab;
Luke 1:26-38 or 1:39-47

Scripture:
A great sign appeared in the sky, a woman clothed with the
sun . . . (Rev 12:1)

Reflection: "It was a beautiful day," Gabriela reminisced. As
refugees from Mexico, she and her family had enthusiasti-
cally anticipated their first American celebration of the Virgin
of Guadalupe. "Tia, my two-year-old, couldn't stop looking
at the special decorations. When the mariachi band started,
her eyes got really big. 'Yes, Our Lady is here in America too.
And she loves our music, just like she did back home!' I told
her. After that she wasn't so shy in church anymore."

You're likely familiar with the apparition of the Virgin
Mary in Mexico (1531) that we celebrate today and with
St. Bernadette's vision in Lourdes (1858). But are you aware
that she has also appeared worldwide, in South America
(Ecuador), the U.S. (Wisconsin), Africa (Rwanda), and Asia
(Japan)?

"Those visitations show us that every single one of us is
always on her radar," a religious sister once assured me as
we discussed this incredible legacy. Then she counseled an
informal Marian practice that I've grown to depend on in

26   *Second Week of Advent*

times of trouble. "When you need Mary," she advised, "dare to imagine that she stands lovingly, gloriously before you. Let go of feelings of unworthiness; picture her. How does she set you at ease? What needs does she anticipate? What does she ask you to do? What special blessing, unique to your culture and circumstances, does she give you?"

What a joy it is today to celebrate this glorious collective Mother, who loves all our songs!

Meditation: Catholics across the world create small shrines, indoors and out, as special places for prayer, adorning them simply with candles, flowers, pictures, etc. Beginning with this season, so full of Mary's presence in Scripture, consider dedicating a space in your home for daily communion with the Blessed Mother, beautifying it with simple objects, and perhaps enhancing your prayer there with music.

Prayer: Holy Mary, Mother of God, pray for me. Hold me always in your loving gaze.

Longing for Light

Readings: Isa 40:25-31; Matt 11:28-30

Scripture:
They that hope in the LORD will renew their strength,
    they will soar as with eagles' wings;
They will run and not grow weary,
    walk and not grow faint. (Isa 40:31)

Reflection: Winter's abbreviated daylight has likely posed a challenge to the mental well-being of humans from the beginning of time. Today we no longer celebrate magic rituals at Stonehenge or offer sacrifices to sun gods, but generic "winter blues" and Seasonal Affective Disorder witness to the still-daunting effect of long winter nights. The sun's brightness offers not just vitamin D and safety from predators, but emotional and spiritual encouragement.

Scandinavian Christians' midwinter celebration of the Feast of St. Lucy speaks with charm and faith-affirming power to this visceral need for light. In the deep winter darkness at that latitude, children process through their communities wearing wreaths of lit candles that echo the crown of light St. Lucy is often depicted wearing. Back home the still-crowned little "Lucies" serve their families coffee and pastries.

What a profound way of remembering the saint, one that emphasizes the ever-present glow of God's promise that Lucy saw. Though blinded, she maintained this "in-sight" despite torture and suffering. The spiritual radiance shining from her crown of sainthood whispers, *Keep the faith. The darkness is but a moment.*

In these shortest days of December, let us draw comfort and courage from what Lucy knew: when darkness threatens, we only need to look to our Savior, warming ourselves in his unfailing glow.

Meditation: Honor Lucy by bringing light to others. What assistance with heavy tasks, patient listening, loving gestures might you offer to someone who's struggling to "keep the faith" despite the darkness of wavering faith or loneliness?

Bring seasonal light into your home too. Program a timer-activated light so your main living space greets you cheerfully each morning or when you arrive home from work; light special candles in the evenings.

Prayer: Loving Christ, take pity on me when my spirit is discouraged by literal or figurative darkness. Help me light others' lives with hope.

Dwelling on Details

Readings: Isa 41:13-20; Matt 11:11-15

Scripture:
I will plant in the desert the cedar,
  acacia, myrtle, and olive . . .
That all may see and know,
  observe and understand,
That the hand of the LORD has done this . . . (Isa 41:19-20)

Reflection: How marvelously Isaiah uses concrete imagery to paint pictures for his listeners! How he invites his listeners' hearts to leap in delight, imagining specific plants' tones of green and gold, their sweet and spicy scents of wood, blooms, and fruit, their balletic twists of branches against the sky, feeling the embodied wonder of God's love.

A teacher friend used to say that students had to be "champion noticers" to write well. They had to become people who were not content with registering a generic scene of "beautiful trees," but who were dedicated to getting the particulars of a scene down in exact detail. Isaiah clearly demonstrates this habit, conveying his contagious reverence for God's created world through his willingness to slow down and notice, to use precise names in evocative litany.

Would that we would always take the time to savor our blessings in such grateful detail. But pressure and haste sometimes blur our eyes, as they did when I caught myself rushing through evening prayer several days ago. "Thanks for letting me do hospice massage today," I intoned—then rather carelessly added, "and for the beautiful sunset." Then, conjuring Isaiah and dedicating myself to a longer session, I slowed down and enumerated specifics with attention that *demonstrated* my gratitude, regaling God with the story of the tiny, trembling woman who relaxed under my hands, the sunset's blazing orange.

The classic advice "Show, don't tell" is as essential for good prayer as it is for good writing.

Meditation: Before you pray tonight, recall a few moments when you especially felt God's touch today. Then recount them in prayer, savoring them lovingly in recollection, letting attention and detail embody your gratefulness.

Prayer: Father of all blessings, all beauty, all kindness given and received, you've extended such grace throughout my day. One moment for which I am especially grateful involved . . .

On Being Satisfied

Readings: Isa 48:17-19; Matt 11:16-19

Scripture:
. . . I, the LORD, your God,
    teach you what is for your good,
    and lead you on the way you should go. (Isa 48:17)

Reflection: It's always so sad—and frustrating—to encounter people who are never satisfied. Whether bosses, employees, strangers, or, God forbid, loved ones, such people threaten to become a contagious source of ingratitude. Try to accommodate them by changing things, and they'll find something new to complain about. If good things happen, they'll find the lead lining. Such behavior isn't simply annoying. As psychologists well know, a long-term habit of naysaying can adversely affect relationships and both mental and physical health.

In today's Gospel Jesus chides skeptical contemporaries who turn a blind eye to John the Baptist's essential message— and his own. Comparing his hearers to grumbling children, he laments that they seem determined to disbelieve, and urges, "Whoever has ears ought to hear" (Matt 11:15).

Pope Francis has identified chronic complaining as a sign of a broken relationship with God. Those whose faith in Jesus' message stands fasts, he writes, will confidently draw on an inner source of consolation when they feel slighted or wronged in earthly circumstances, knowing that God will abundantly protect and nourish them in all the ways that matter.

Would that the most discontent among us could perceive the overflowing cup of blessings God offers so freely for the taking. Would that the rest of us might buoy them up with constant rejoicing, with faith grounded in the assurance that good things are our destiny!

Teach us such things for our good, O God, even now.

Meditation: If you feel yourself slipping into chronic dissatisfaction, cultivate an Advent practice of attentiveness to signs of grace. You might jot quick observations of blessings in a small pocket notebook and draw on them for the detail-oriented prayer described in yesterday's meditation. If someone you love is gratitude-challenged, add a "today's good things" sharing component to your family dinner conversation (nobody gets to pass!).

Prayer: Help me recognize my pasture's abundance, O Shepherd Christ, whenever dissatisfaction beckons.

December 16: Saturday of the Second Week of Advent

Marvelous Healing

Readings: Sir 48:1-4, 9-11; Matt 17:9a, 10-13

Scripture:
You were destined, it is written, in time to come
    to put an end to wrath before the day of the LORD,
To turn back the hearts of fathers toward their sons . . .
    (Sir 48:10)

Reflection: "Forgiving is the hardest thing for so many people," my young counselor friend says as we enjoy a weekend walk together. "Especially at this time of year." Without breaking confidence, she speaks of families still divided by harsh words spoken, painful deeds done long ago. "And the closer parents and children were, the harder it often is for them to forgive."

I nod, thinking of my own past struggles to forgive those I love, even when the hurt they inflicted was not deliberate. I remind myself to keep working lovingly toward reconciliation in one relationship not utterly broken, yet tarnished by self-protecting distrust.

How marvelous it is then—in a literal sense—when today's Scripture invites us to trust that the King of Love will eventually heal all such wounds, though they may seem to us tragically doomed to fester.

And even more amazing it is to realize that our Father, God, isn't waiting for the end-times to extend forgiveness to us, despite our ongoing tendency to speak harsh words and perform wounding acts. All we have to do is seek reconciliation now, and the arms open wide.

Granted, it's the rare human being who can even approximate such marvelous clemency. Given our nature, it's hard to let hurt feelings go and again become vulnerable. But in the spirit of love, the theme of the Advent week just ahead, we owe it to ourselves and those we love to try.

Meditation: Call to mind divisions in your own life. Who has wronged you? Whom have you wronged? Choose one situation and pray that your heart may be set free of all wrath or festering hurt. Take specific steps: When you catch yourself nurturing bitterness, deliberately change your thoughts by recalling and celebrating the good times you've had with that person. Imagine ways you might make amends, or what a true, loving apology or expression of forgiveness might sound like, word for word. Don't rush. Entertain various possibilities, getting used to this healing orientation. When the time is right, reach out.

Prayer: Prince of Peace, stay by my side as I seek to reconcile with those I love.

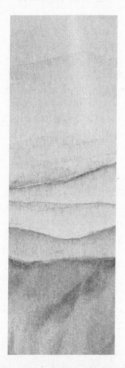

THIRD WEEK OF ADVENT

December 17: Third Sunday of Advent

Choosing Joy

Readings: Isa 61:1-2a, 10-11; 1 Thess 5:16-24; John 1:6-8, 19-28

Scripture:
[I]n my God is the joy of my soul . . . (Isa 61:10)

Reflection: "It's Pink Sunday!" the little girl exclaimed, twirling after Mass in her fluffy dress of that hue. "You're wearing the best color, Father!" she congratulated the priest who'd been chatting with me. "And my Mommy's making a pink cake for tonight!"

The proper term for this third Sunday in Advent, of course, is Gaudete Sunday, from the Latin word meaning "rejoice." In earlier centuries it offered reprieve from Lent-like Advent disciplines; today it still encourages smiles as we light our wreaths' third candles in happy anticipation of the ever-nearer celebration of Christ's birth.

Expressing joy as we do today has a venerable place in Christian worship. No less a figure than scholar and theologian St. Thomas Aquinas—the kind of man one might expect to counsel against frivolity—spoke warmly in its favor. For Aquinas joy constituted an outward sign of faith, evidence of a soul's charitable disposition and love for God. Holy cheer was a virtue, he wrote, one to be actively cultivated as an "operative habit," even a Christian duty.

So let us discard any sense that we should not be "too happy" before Christmas Day arrives. Let us, on this "Pink Sunday," bask, even revel, in divine love.

Meditation: A character in one of singer-songwriter Joni Mitchell's songs speaks of "sacrific[ing] . . . blues" as a prerequisite for seeking human love. That line helped save my life during a period of suicidal thoughts years ago, inspiring me to radically give over my grief and depression to God, asking from the depths of my pain to be infused with the comfort and joy of divine love.

Is sadness or a sense of unworthiness preventing you from joining the church's celebration today? Ask God to help you find a quiet joy deep in your heart.

Prayer: Loving God, may a gentle spirit of joy fill and heal my heart today.

December 18: Monday of the Third Week of Advent

Supporting Characters

Readings: Jer 23:5-8; Matt 1:18-25

Scripture:
When Joseph awoke, he did as the angel of the Lord had commanded him. (Matt 1:24)

Reflection: St. Joseph is among the most beloved saints, declared patron of the universal church by Pope Pius IX in 1870, addressed in special prayers, and recently honored with a church year specially devoted to him (2021).

Though the Bible is short on details about this exemplary man's life, what we do know demonstrates richly varied virtue. Today's Gospel highlights Joseph's obedience, his compassionate heart, and his attentiveness to God's direction. Other stories demonstrate his good citizenship in complying with the census, resourceful courage on the flight to Egypt, and fatherly concern seeking the lost Jesus in the temple.

Arguably Joseph's most amazing virtue, though, is humility, manifested in willingness to play the role of supporting character in Jesus' and Mary's story. What a wonderful everyday precedent this gentle trait sets for the rest of us, who will routinely find ourselves inconvenienced or unnoticed in the role of "support staff" in jobs, marriages, friendships, and parenting.

Perhaps you know or are a Joseph at this very moment, confronted with demands stemming from a dependent's circumstances. Such "Josephs" spend long hours driving loved ones to medical appointments and caregiving at home. They work overtime to support families when the Holy Spirit has inspired spouses to return to school or embrace a call to lower-paying but meaningful employment. They listen to friends in crisis and drive children to piano lessons. They graciously offer praise, letting others shine.

Oh you just ones, your reward will be great in heaven!

Meditation: In whose story are you acting as a supporting character? Who's playing that part in yours? Ask Joseph to bless all who make others' paths easier and to help helpers grow in selflessness and love.

Prayer: God of Joseph, let me embrace humble service as a noble vocation.

December 19: Tuesday of the Third Week of Advent

Whatever You Ask . . . with a Twist

Readings: Judg 13:2-7, 24-25a; Luke 1:5-25

Scripture:
"Though you are barren and have had no children, yet you will conceive and bear a son." (Judg 13:3)

Reflection: Elizabeth must have been so delighted to hear the news of her pregnancy. In ancient Israel offspring meant respect and status, proof of God's favor, family continuity, parents' security in old age. She and her husband had been waiting so long that hope had faded.

But Elizabeth and Zechariah's son wouldn't have been what they expected—not a dutiful "regular" son but a prophet and desert-dweller living on locusts and wild honey, shaking up the establishment. Artists have fancifully suggested that John the Baptist displayed unconventionality even as an infant, painting him as wide-eyed, restless, and larger than your average baby, wearing a cute little animal-skin "onesie" as he plays with his cousin Jesus.

Perhaps that's going too far, but given how personality manifests in childhood, it seems fair to assume that he may have been a handful. Proud as the devout Elizabeth and Zechariah must have been, they may from time to time have wished for a "normal," boring son. Yet it was through this unconventional child that the two found a timeless legacy of renown and honor.

"Ask and it will be given to you," Jesus assures us. And ask we should, and do, as Elizabeth and Zechariah did—though it's always best to anticipate that God might have his own ideas about just how that request plays out!

Meditation: Can you remember how you responded to the news that you were going to have a child (or to the dawning recognition that you might become a close influencer to someone else's child as a godparent, mentor, friend, or favorite teacher)? What were your early wishes or expectations for that young one? Has the reality evolved differently, in ways that seem to bear God's signature? Meditate on the divine wisdom that shapes each of us for purposes that serve an end we mortals cannot always anticipate.

Prayer: Give me faith and strength, God of Mystery, when circumstances turn out differently than I anticipated.

Ready to Greet Him

Readings: Isa 7:10-14; Luke 1:26-38

Scripture:
The angel said to her, "Do not be afraid, Mary." (Luke 1:30)

Reflection: Today's Gospel returns to the annunciation, reminding us that this rich narrative has layers that blossom with multiple readings. In this case such deeper insight is invited by the contrast between the first reading and the Gospel, both of which depict responses to a messenger of God.

While both Ahaz the king, in the first instance, and Mary the young woman, in the second, receive momentous news, their consciences prompt vastly different reactions. Conscious of his own unresolved sin (betraying Judah in an Assyrian alliance and permitting pagan shrines), Ahaz—clearly nervous—tries to wiggle out of speaking to God. Mary, "full of grace" and free of any sense of having offended the Lord, embraces the angel's message and God's will.

Truth time: Given your own conscience, how would you respond if a messenger from God materialized before you right now? We'd all like to imagine ourselves as pure enough that, like Mary, we'd quickly agree to whatever was being asked of us in God's name. But speaking for myself, I can remember more than one occasion when, if that had happened to me, my conscience would have shivered, and I might have croaked, "Could you come back again tomorrow?"

What is the state of your conscience as we prepare to celebrate Christ's birth? Are you aware, like Ahaz, of having wearied God?

Even now the first echoes of those trumpets sound: *He is the king of glory.* Now is definitely the time to ready ourselves to greet him.

Meditation: God can always tell when we're "spiritually off"—and our own hearts can too. Use the next few days to frankly examine your conscience and take advantage of the sacrament of reconciliation, so that your "Yes!" will ring out joyfully at Christmas.

Prayer: Create in me a clean heart, O God, that I may be free of fear as I welcome your coming.

December 21: Thursday of the Third Week of Advent

True Love

Readings: Song 2:8-14 or Zeph 3:14-18a; Luke 1:39-45

Scripture:
"For at the moment the sound of your greeting reached my ears, the infant in my womb leaped for joy." (Luke 1:44)

Reflection: Whose mere presence makes your heart leap with delight? Is it a spouse or significant other, parent or child, dear friend . . . or, lucky you, several of the above?

What qualities in a person inspire such an effect? In the beginning the thrill of romantic love might well be sparked by physical beauty, which today's first reading so gloriously evokes as a lover "springing across the mountains" (Song 2:8). But if that first question brought dear faces to mind—and I pray it did—you already know that enduring love flows from deeper wells. Not based on illusion or projection, it persists despite the misunderstandings that plague friendships, marriages, and parent-child relationships alike, admiring the best in the loved one. It respects differences and seeks the other's growth. It delights in the other's delight. It's at once comfortably steady and always growing.

Today's Scriptures encourage us to imagine such marvelous, faithful love embodied in divine presence. The stunning love poetry in the Song of Songs is often interpreted as an allegory of Christ's love for his bride, the church; Luke's

Gospel demonstrates how instinctive it is for the faithful to delight in Christ's presence.

Is your heart continuing to leap with last Sunday's joy as you ready yourself to celebrate love perfected? How can you share that joy with the human beings you love?

Meditation: Take time to meditate on Christ as an ideal lover, brother, or friend. How has he worked to bring out the best in you, invited you to dream big, and helped you grow in faith toward unity with him? What flaws has he forgiven, time and again? How has he inspired you to trust in your mutual love? Pray with rejoicing; perhaps write a love poem to him.

Prayer: Help me ever to rest secure in your glorious, persistent faith in me, Loving Christ.

Gifts, Multiplied

Readings: 1 Sam 1:24-28; Luke 1:46-56

Scripture:
"Now I, in turn, give him to the LORD; as long as he lives, he shall be dedicated to the LORD." (Sam 1:28)

Reflection: I'll always remember my surprise when Cecelia (let's call her) invited me to join her in leading music at Mass. Cecelia's voice is amazing, a rich mezzo-soprano with an enormous range and beautiful timber. Mine is trained but nothing special, morphed by age to a limited alto-going-on-tenor. Not only did that invitation warm my heart, it also inspired me to learn to sing harmony—something I'd long imagined but never done—in hopes of contributing something new.

Ten years along, I've come to realize that Cecelia's capacity for generosity is as predictable and rich as her singing ability. It shone during her career as an accountant, when she worked through breaks and lunch hours to earn time off for singing at funerals. Now retired, she spends many hours decorating the church, organizing the music ministry, etc. She's also a ready and sympathetic counselor to those who flock instinctively to her, approaching after Mass to request a few minutes now, a morning later.

How wonderfully Cecelia multiplies God's gifts, open-handedly sharing energy and resources with the community, as Hannah did. Like Mary's "yes," her selflessness offers a channel for grace and blessings needed by others, riches ever renewing from the Source of all good things.

What are you giving to your community this Christmas? What are you giving to God?

Meditation: Do you know a "Cecelia" whose generosity with God-given gifts makes an enormous difference, inspiring others to marvel at the holy goodness that creates such people? Pray in thanksgiving—but also remember that although these givers might seem always joyful, like everybody else they're subject to burnout, hidden exhaustion, and self-doubt. They are making sacrifices to give what they have.

Find a way to support these givers in your life. Voicing affirmation is good; volunteering to employ your own gifts to assume part of the responsibilities they carry is even better.

Prayer: I raise my voice in thanks today, generous God, for all the givers. Bless them richly this Christmas and always.

December 23: Saturday of the Third Week of Advent

Abiding in Hope

Readings: Mal 3:1-4, 23-24; Luke 1:57-66

Scripture:
But who will endure the day of his coming?
   And who can stand when he appears?
For he is like the refiner's fire,
   or like the fuller's lye. (Mal 3:2)

Reflection: Perhaps I was an overly serious child and remain a too-serious adult, but while counting myself among the multitudes who love the "Hallelujah" chorus in Handel's *Messiah*, so often performed during this Christmas season, I've always found a much shorter piece to be the most moving. The song ("But who may abide the day of His coming?") is a repetition of a single verse from today's reading from the prophet Malachi.

Appearing near the composition's beginning (in what we might call the "Advent section"), this musical moment is proclaimed by a single, darkly beautiful voice. It appears as an abrupt contrast (a major "oh, oh" moment, my college choral director once called it), interrupting expressions of enthusiastic joy over the prospect of valleys being exalted with a sudden reality check: that day will also bring judgment.

The question of "who will endure" remains a very good one. In our era as in Handel's eighteenth-century context, after all, no matter how many "Hallelujahs" we proclaim, we remain sinners. Our awareness of this may have us quaking! Yet our faith instills hope, proclaiming that our Savior loves us and will extend unimaginable, unearned grace to those who follow him. Rather than obsessing over the impossibility of being "worthy," we are called to keep the commandments, serve others, repent when we falter, and trust in Christ's promises.

Yes, we may still need to be refined "like gold or like silver" (Mal 3:3). But the results are going to feel marvelous, indeed.

Who may abide? Actually, all who love the Savior and keep his ways.

Meditation: Imagine that the Lord has "come suddenly to his temple" (Mal 3:1) and the time for judgment has arrived. In the "Hallelujah" spirit, picture the aspects of your life where God will "meet [you] doing right" (Isa 64:4) and give thanks for them. Now acknowledge the places where a touch of refining is still needed, and give thanks for grace.

Prayer: Merciful Christ, let me anticipate your coming with grateful, humble, hopeful trust.

FOURTH WEEK OF ADVENT

December 24: Fourth Sunday of Advent

Practicing Peace

Readings: 2 Sam 7:1-5, 8b-12, 14a, 16; Rom 16:25-27;
Luke 1:26-38

Scripture:
. . . I will plant them so that they may dwell in their place
without further disturbance. (2 Sam 7:10)

Reflection: Peace—celebrated with today's final Advent
candle—is surely among the conditions most necessary for
human flourishing. When a land is racked by war or instabil-
ity, people can't focus on raising families, working produc-
tively, or serving God. On a micro level, fight-or-flight
hormones flood our bodies when we're stressed, raising
blood pressure, blighting sleep, and making us fretful and
anxious.

It's natural that our souls soar, then, at the proclamation
of divinely ordained peace in today's Gospel. Ironically, this
year's fourth Sunday of Advent falls on Christmas Eve, when
cultivating peace may prove especially challenging. For
many people December 24 is frantic and pressured; lines are
long and tempers short; there's a last-minute rush to shop,
wrap, decorate, prepare food. If you look around at Christmas Eve Mass, you'll surely see some exhausted, distracted
faces.

That was my reality, anyway, until a few years ago when my spiritual advisor offered stellar advice: treat December 24 as a day of holy leisure from stress-producing activities. Prioritize and pre-plan essentials throughout December, she suggested; be brutally realistic about what's possible, and vow that anything not done by 9:00 p.m. on December 23 is expendable. Plan something enjoyable, low-key, and non-negotiable with friends or family on December 24—an outdoor excursion, a cooking or decorating party—and reserve some solo time to meditate on Advent's lessons.

How can we find Christmas Eve peace? I'm here to tell you that if you "rest beside the weary road" on this sacred day (to echo the old carol, "It Came Upon a Midnight Clear"), you just might be able, now and then, to "hear the angels sing."

Meditation: How can you cultivate peace amid today's busyness in your heart and home? Can you let someone else (or yourself) off the hook for a particular holiday expectation? What kind of individual or collective break would help you or your loved ones cultivate a peaceful spirit today?

Prayer: Jesus, you said to your disciples, "Peace be with you" (John 20:19). Slow my pace and calm my heart today. Ready me to focus my whole being on greeting you.

SEASON OF CHRISTMAS

December 25: The Nativity of the Lord (Christmas)

Great Joy to All People

Readings:
VIGIL: Isa 62:1-5; Acts 13:16-17, 22-25; Matt 1:1-25 or
     1:18-25
NIGHT: Isa 9:1-6; Titus 2:11-14; Luke 2:1-14
DAWN: Isa 62:11-12; Titus 3:4-7; Luke 2:15-20
DAY: Isa 52:7-10; Heb 1:1-6; John 1:1-18 or 1:1-5, 9-14

Scripture:
Sing joyfully to the LORD, all you lands;
  break into song; sing praise. (Ps 98:4)

Reflection: After all the waiting, all the preparing, our festal
day has come! Perhaps you're reading this still groggy from
sleep after midnight Mass. Or maybe you've just returned
from an early Christmas Day service. Perhaps you're the
only one awake in your house, basking in the chance to be
alone with God. Or maybe you're turning to prayer after
eating a festive breakfast and opening gifts. Whatever the
case, how marvelous it is that—on a day when happy chaos
can prove so distracting—you've set aside time to reflect on
the Source of all our joy.

As you do, let your happiness be multiplied by calling to
mind the community of Christians across the globe. Millions
unified in faith are even now celebrating this great feast, and
millions have celebrated before us, passing down their

celebratory traditions to us. Just as the ancient "O Come, O Come, Emmanuel" echoes throughout our Advent, Christmas songs with deep historical roots enliven modern celebrations. The tune for "What Child Is This?" ("Greensleeves") originated in the 1500s, with Christmas lyrics added in the late 1600s; "While Shepherds Watched Their Flocks by Night" was written in 1700. Seasonal greenery has decorated houses for at least six hundred years. Our long-departed brothers and sisters in faith would even find much to recognize in today's Christmas Mass.

I don't know about you, but thinking about such continuity gives me chills of wonder. What a testimony to human longing for God's mercy, for death's vanquishing! What a comfort to be one among such a multitude of believers who've accepted Christ's promise, trusting that they'll greet him when he comes again—and meet each other in his kingdom.

Praise God from whom all blessings flow . . . especially this blessing of Christmas.

Meditation: Pay special attention today to the intergenerational family Christmas customs that color your celebration. Remember and pray for those who originated, enjoyed, and passed down those distinctive traditions.

Prayer: Eternal God, accept my song of joy today, as you've accepted so many others.

Illuminating the Season

Readings: Acts 6:8-10; 7:54-59; Matt 10:17-22

Scripture:
He, filled with the Holy Spirit, looked up intently to heaven and saw the glory of God and Jesus standing at the right hand of God. (Acts 7:56)

Reflection: Call me old-fashioned, but I wince at the sight of bedraggled Christmas trees stacked at curbs as trash on December 26. For those who so tacitly proclaim, *So over that!*, the feast heralded with such excitement is decisively finished for another year. December's sense of community, its seasonal license for expressing love and appreciation that remains unvoiced at other times of year, has dissolved into the ordinary world once again. How long is it until the Super Bowl?

What a difference we find in our churches, as the true Christmas season is properly beginning. Our freshly erected trees and candles still shine; poinsettias now compound the brightness of the altar; shepherds and the baby Jesus have appeared at the manger. We have fourteen more days to revel in this season uniquely set apart for remembering our Lord's birth, for marveling at the signs of grace that marked his earliest years.

Let us honor this feast by extending December's loving customs, keeping our spirits bright, renewing our hope even as the world around us lets that spirit fade.

And even after our extended celebration is past, let us hold close to our hearts what Stephen knew: that those who "[look] up intently to heaven" with faith can experience our God's bright love on any day of the year.

Meditation: Consider introducing new rituals into your home to mark the beginning of the Christmas season. The stories of Jesus' youth might inspire yearly children's games and crafts. The readings' references to splendor might prompt the addition of bright home decorations reserved for post-Advent celebration. You might even honor ancient tradition by planning a festive gathering in honor of this year's "Epiphany Eve" or "Twelfth Night," the last of the twelve days of Christmas.

Prayer: Ever-radiant Christ, help my heart stay fresh through all the days of Christmas, my faith remain brightly contagious.

With Our Own Eyes

Readings: 1 John 1:1-4; John 20:1a, 2-8

Scripture:
What we have seen with our own eyes . . . concerns the
Word of life . . . that was with the Father and was made
visible to us. (1 John 1:1-2)

Reflection: As a health-care worker specializing in elder care,
Sarah had long considered herself skilled in comforting
people in crisis. When her own aged mother lost physical-
mental ground, however, she discovered that she could not
offer herself the consolation that she'd so often extended to
others. Consumed by anxiety, she found her heart racing,
sleep fleeting, attention scattered.

As the end neared, though, consolation came to her from
the dying woman herself, a person of abiding faith. I was
privileged to attend the older woman's final hours, offering
music therapy and comforting touch, marveling at her peace
with what was happening. Her passing—one breath, then
not another—brought something sacred, mysterious, enfold-
ingly secure into the room, a peace that we all felt.

A crusading atheist who writes for our local paper recently
taunted believers with naivete regarding belief in an afterlife.
Nothing but "old stories" from unreliable witnesses (like the
disciples) support hope for resurrection, he pronounced.

Only a weakling or a fool would go gentle into that good night.

As a hospice worker, I beg to differ. For nearly ten years, I've watched members of Christ's Body greeting the great transition with secure tranquility. They seem to know much more at that point than the rest of us about what lies ahead, and their responses suggest anything but despair.

Christ's resurrection may have occurred millennia ago, but there's still plenty of visible evidence to assure us that our "joy may be complete" (1 John 1:4).

Meditation: If fear of death haunts you, studying our faith's perspective on death and aging can help. Catholic websites offer courses; recent books provide a thoughtful, uplifting perspective (see References at the end of this book for a few suggestions). Speaking with a minister to the dying (or shadowing one) can offer meaningful insights.

Prayer: When I quake with the fear that I'll cease to exist, O Lord, comfort me with evidence of eternal love made visible, that I too may proclaim the resurrection.

Transforming Pity into Love

Readings: 1 John 1:5–2:2; Matt 2:13-18

Scripture:
"A voice was heard in Ramah,
sobbing and loud lamentation . . ." (Matt 2:18)

Reflection: In my "first act" career as a professor, I was blessed to work with young adults motivated by high aspirations and an incredible work ethic. This was not at an elite university but an open admissions state school, and most of these students were first-generation college attendees relying on both financial aid and part-time employment.

So I've been surprised and concerned in recent years when, as a traveling health-care worker visiting patients in their homes, I've encountered many young people who seem to be drifting. I've heard difficult stories from parents, too, of drugs and other heartbreaking addictions and decisions that stand between their children and the future their parents dream of for them. It goes without saying that this is happening in homes that represent all demographics of class, ethnicity, and faith—in homes where parents have done everything humanly possible to raise healthy, curious, engaged children.

Sometimes troubled or unhappy kids need adult role models beyond their parents. Aunts, uncles, and grandparents used to provide those listening ears and guiding voices, but today they often live far away.

And that's where we can come in, on this Feast of the Holy Innocents and all year long. We'll naturally honor the day by praying for vulnerable children worldwide, but we mustn't forget the children in our own towns and cities who could use the direction and support our friendship and attention might provide. There are so many ways we can help: through one-on-one mentor programs, by volunteering at a youth center or after-school program, by becoming a scout leader or partnering with a school to lead a new interest group.

Such work can be very challenging, yes. But through it we just might—figuratively or literally—save a life.

Meditation: Instead of judging young people who are struggling—*that one's a bad seed*—we can educate ourselves about opportunities in our communities to volunteer, serve, and support. Transforming theoretical disapproval or pity into active love is a wonderful way to celebrate today's feast.

Prayer: Compassionate Christ, may today's Gospel move me to serve children far and near.

Little Stumbles, Serious Sin

Readings: 1 John 2:3-11; Luke 2:22-35

Scripture:
Whoever says he is in the light, yet hates his brother, is still in the darkness. (1 John 2:9)

Reflection: I like to believe that hatred is not among my bosom sins. I rarely hold grudges; typically, I'm angry at myself, not others. But today's readings echo with ominous relevance as I recall an occurrence just a few days ago.

How rude I was, though at the time I excused myself. All I'd wanted to do was put away the music stands. While singing for Christmas Eve Mass is a blessing, it's also a long commitment, what with practice earlier in the day, carols before the service, and a good deal of music during. I was so ready to go home. But large family groups of people I'd never seen before had swarmed the altar, snapping pictures with our parish's hand-carved manger scene.

"Excuse me!" I blurted. When they didn't move, I brusquely nudged.

The steps are short from self-absorption to resentment to hatred, and I'd definitely advanced along that path. Had grace lived in me, I might have delighted in this inconvenient crowd's foray into church, made them feel at home. Instead,

I became a poster person for unwelcoming, self-righteous church ladies.

The term "mortal sin" typically brings to mind big, splashy falls. But the careless little ego-driven stumbles that separate us, even momentarily, from our King of Love, can prove dangerous in their own way too.

Meditation: Notice your interactions with others, even casual interactions, during the remaining days of Christmas. Note where self-absorption or busy-ness leads you to be less than charitable. Vow to catch this sin before it happens and substitute behavior reflecting Christ's loving spirit. Consider reinforcing this habit-building by recording your experiences in a written journal.

Prayer: Make me a channel of your peace, O Lord. Where there is hatred—including hatred nestling in my own heart—help me cultivate your love.

Models for Coping with Unexpected Change

Readings: 1 John 2:12-17; Luke 2:36-40

Scripture:
[She] lived seven years with her husband . . . and then as a widow until she was eighty-four. (Luke 2:36-37)

Reflection: As a widow myself, I wish we knew more about the widowed Anna's life, in particular how she came to hear the call to spend days and nights in the temple, praying and praising God as what Luke calls "a prophetess" (2:36). I imagine her feeling lost after her husband's death. Yet grace led her to a radically new vocation. Instead of taking a catastrophic turn, her life became deeply satisfying though different from what she'd imagined, one of beautiful service to God and others.

If you've ever found your own expectations about the future abruptly upended in any way, Anna offers a powerful model. We don't know the details of her journey; almost certainly the way would have been bumpy, anguished. Yet Anna clearly discovered—as those of us displaced today by a loved one's death, a job's end, financial crisis, disability, or illness—that openness to where God leads is more life-giving than refusing to move forward.

When life is sailing along as planned, it's comforting to know that when "normal" is disrupted, as inevitably will happen, holy ones like Anna and the multitude of saints whose vocations involved a radical change of plans (Ignatius of Loyola, Elizabeth Seton, Maximilian Kolbe) are waiting to be our guides.

Meditation: What circumstances in your life are impossible to imagine changing? Open your mind to the possibility that those circumstances may be stages in a complex and varied plan. That doesn't mean not loving this day, these people, this work. It does mean, though, making peace with the reality that at some point, you too may be called to an unexpected tomorrow.

Prayer: Shepherd me, O God, when the death of expectations upsets my world. Help me move beyond my hopes and fears into rich new pastures.

December 31: The Holy Family of Jesus, Mary, and Joseph

Loving Our Imperfect, Holy Families

Readings: Sir 3:2-6, 12-14; Col 3:12-21 or 3:12-17; Luke 2:22-40
or 2:22, 39-40

Scripture:
Put on . . . heartfelt compassion, kindness, humility, gentleness, and patience, bearing with one another and forgiving one another . . . (Col 3:12-13)

Reflection: Have you ever found yourself brooding about less-than-perfect behavior at a family Christmas celebration? If so, you're in vast company, for whether the "family" gathered was nuclear, extended, or a group of friends, many human beings have difficulty behaving perfectly on holidays—or on any days!

I recently came across a painting of the Holy Family that, while pretty, feeds unrealistic expectations. It depicts Jesus, Mary, and Joseph on the flight to Egypt as relaxed, perfectly groomed travelers, smiling on a clean road among orderly flocks and polite shepherds. Even the sheep are sparkling clean.

Yes, the subtext is presumably their absolute trust in God. But come on! How hurried and anxious Herod's deadly threat must have made this family, the stress no doubt etched on their faces. The way would have been rough, fellow travelers impolite, clothes soon muddy or dusty, the air loud with the sounds of people and animals, thick with noxious scents.

A less beautiful picture? Undeniably. But ultimately a more helpful one, I believe, as we go through life with our own very real families. Staying holy in the face of messy challenges, this take on Jesus' family implies that there might just be hope for our families too.

Consider this: Paul would not have advised the Colossians to bear with each other if "bearing" weren't obviously called for, if he didn't believe that ordinary mortals could succeed in forming sacred relationships.

Meditation: With a forgiving spirit, meditate or journal about less-than-perfect moments during your family's recent celebrations. Move quickly from documenting to reflecting on what features of the metaphorical road's dust, dirt, and stresses might have prompted others to act as they did. Let resentment go. Affirm love.

Prayer: God of love, may my thoughts, words, and deeds always work to affirm the holiness of my own imperfect, beautiful family.

Taking the Time to Ponder

Readings: Num 6:22-27; Gal 4:4-7; Luke 2:16-21

Scripture:
And Mary kept all these things, reflecting on them in her heart. (Luke 2:19)

Reflection: "Reflecting" (or "pondering") might seem like a quaint, outdated process given today's emphasis on efficient decisiveness. Online contacts demand answers within minutes; self-help gurus warn against prolonged decision-making. "Overthinking is dangerous," I read last week on a blog designed for small business owners. According to its upbeat author, "analysis paralysis" courts failure and implies weak character. If you find yourself "dithering," the article counsels, immediately embrace simple, snap-out-of-it tips: set a two-minute deadline for making sense of a quandary, try thinking "black and white."

Mary, thank heavens, knew better. So does the centuries-long fraternity of monastics and spiritual seekers who have practiced *lectio divina*. Perhaps you're among them, having learned the art on retreat or in a workshop, or by using a Bible study text that encourages deeper contemplation. Though a naturally speedy person, I too now know better, having learned while writing reflections like this one that if I read a day's text and then immediately begin composing, what emerges is lackluster at best. Only through "incubation" in the patient spirit of pondering—studying a text, then simply being with it for hours or days, learning to trust subconscious connections, daily serendipity, and the Holy Spirit's whispers—can inspiration evolve and deepen.

Two minutes? Some mysteries demand a lifetime of attention if we're even to begin to appreciate their magnificent subtlety, their loving nuance.

Meditation: Popular culture pegs New Year's Day as a time for making firm resolutions. Yet such intentions' formulaic nature usually dooms them. In the spirit of Mary's reflecting, instead take your time to ponder the year just concluded, reflecting on where your conscience is satisfied or unsatisfied. Ask patiently for guidance regarding how to better serve the Mystery in the months ahead. Listen. Follow.

Prayer: When the pressure mounts to speak or decide too quickly, help me remember, O Lord, that the first thought is seldom the best thought. Help me wait for the Holy Spirit's voice.

Acknowledging the Source

Readings: 1 John 2:22-28; John 1:19-28

Scripture:
"Who are you, so we can give an answer to those who sent us?" (John 1:22)

Reflection: No wonder John the Baptist is asked to identify himself. He has no credentials. He isn't a "regular" in the temple. But he's preaching and baptizing, and his desert ministry is getting a lot of attention.

An earlier reflection in this book mentioned the baby John's distinctive character in Renaissance art. The same holds true for depictions of him as an adult. If what John's questioners saw even remotely approached what the painters imagined, no wonder they had questions! In painting after painting, while others stand dignified in their robes, John is inevitably disheveled, sunburned, barefooted, long-haired like a hippie lurking at the group's edge. Succeeding at a "Where's John?" Waldo-style search game in Italian art galleries is a no-brainer.

Today we might say that John had a definite "brand"—considered a good thing for entrepreneurs and entertainers—a niched identity that's a claim to fame.

Yet when John's pinned down, he promotes not himself, but Christ. Deflecting any personal distinction, he praises the one who is to come, giving credit where it's due.

What's your "brand" in the faith community? Are you the one who works with disabled children, the one who keeps the church linens looking so pristine, the parish council workhorse?

It feels good to be recognized, certainly. But let us, like John, ultimately give glory to the God who formed us for his service.

Meditation: Vow in this new year to acknowledge God's grace in every worthy thing you're called to offer up. Practice marveling on the spot when something helpful flows from your hand. Thank God humbly each evening for the day's opportunities to manifest your gifts.

Prayer: May the distinction in which I take greatest pride, O God, be my eagerness to serve you.

Imagining Heaven

Readings: 1 John 2:29–3:6; John 1:29-34

Scripture:
What we shall be has not yet been revealed . . . for we shall
see him as he is. (1 John 3:2)

Reflection: Strange as it may seem today, readers of popular
novels in nineteenth-century America loved stories set in
heaven. Spurred by the runaway success of Elizabeth Stuart
Phillips' *The Gates Ajar* (1868), eighty works of fiction fol-
lowed, depicting the dead living in houses, raising families,
playing games. Heaven, readers were reassured, would be
just like earth, only more pleasant.

While widespread bereavement from the Civil War helps
explain this particular craze, afterlife fiction has found enthusiastic audiences in many times and places, its examples
stretching from Dante's *Divine Comedy* to today's *The Lovely
Bones*. We're a species that likes to be able to anticipate what's
coming—and what could be more fascinating to pin down
than our posthumous fate?

Imagining heaven is a pretty harmless activity, so long as
we heed John's caution and remember that, comforting as
they might be, specific projections are sorely limited, just like
our characterizations of God as an aged, white-bearded man.

Still, it seems to me that anything that encourages joyful anticipation is good. An old gospel song catches that happy spirit: "In the sweet by and by, / We shall meet on that beautiful shore."

So let us vow to patiently wait and see, trusting that though we cannot map that land's precise topography, we can certainly count on its sweetness.

Meditation: Cultivate your own yearning for heaven by revisiting a favorite piece of literature, music, or art that depicts the afterlife, though admittedly "through a glass, darkly" (1 Cor 13:12; KJV). If you're so inclined, record your own imaginings in a work of art or share them with a trusted friend.

Prayer: Help me to wait in joyful hope, faithful God, for the time when I shall be changed, confident that all shall be well beyond my imagining.

January 4: Saint Elizabeth Ann Seton

Braving a Revolutionary Path

Readings: 1 John 3:7-10; John 1:35-42

Scripture:
The person who acts in righteousness is righteous. (1 John 3:7)

Reflection: If you see a portrait of Elizabeth Ann Seton without knowing her backstory, you might assume she was a conventional woman of her early American era. Dressed decorously, looking virtuous and well-behaved, she seems unlikely to have shaken up anything.

In fact, Seton was a revolutionary, a woman of nonconformist ideas whose brave, selfless, faith-driven action deeply impacted education and women's possibilities for religious life in America. So extraordinary was that quiet-looking woman that she became our country's first saint.

Born in 1774 to a prosperous Anglican New York family, Seton initially seemed destined for a contented life as wife, mother, and altruist—until she tragically lost her husband. Declining remarriage, at age twenty-eight she shocked her social circle and alienated her family by converting to Catholicism (then considered a religion of poor immigrants). She embraced public service, establishing schools for girls in Baltimore and on the Maryland frontier (now Mount

St. Mary's University). She also founded the American Sisters of Charity.

Choosing a life path unimaginable for a girl of her upbringing, Seton served God as an innovative leader. Her forward-thinking schools endorsed girls' capacity as people of faith and reason; her mentoring of female teachers formed a generation of principled servants. Enduring illness, loved ones' deaths, discouragement, opposition, and controversy, she modeled heroic conviction.

"By their fruits you will know them" (Matt 7:16). In this case the lesson is clear: brave righteousness comes in many different packages, indeed.

Meditation: What norms do you believe need shaking up if God's kingdom on earth is to be strengthened? Is fear of being judged "out there" keeping you from taking steps to challenge dehumanizing limitations? Let the Holy Spirit guide you in discernment; brainstorm ways you can start to make a difference as Elizabeth Seton did—even a small, local difference.

Prayer: Heavenly Father, give me the courage to follow your call beyond my comfort zone, doing my part to help your kingdom come.

January 5: Saint John Neumann

Holiness in Ordinary Places

Readings: 1 John 3:11-21; John 1:43-51

Scripture:
"Can anything good come from Nazareth?" (John 1:46)

Reflection: While the community where I live would dwarf the tiny village of Nazareth, outsiders from hipper parts of the state consider it, too, an uncultured backwater. Even long-term residents assume it's natural that the "famous" people born here—professional athletes, actors, a Peloton yoga instructor—would invariably move away. Recently I heard someone marvel that our parish's resident theologian, a man in demand nationally for workshops, would choose to live contentedly here.

What a sorry way to regard one's own nest! As history so amply demonstrates, extraordinary people can appear anywhere—like Francis, born in the hamlet of Assisi, or St. Isidore the farmer, who spent an entire life in the sticks near Madrid . . . or Jesus, of Nazareth. If we believe that wonders come only from distant places, we'll miss so much, like the hypothetical Siena neighbor who might have grinned, "Oh, that's just crazy Catherine, the dyer's daughter."

Fortunately God finds ways to encourage us to pay attention to his holy ones, no matter where they're born or live.

In Jesus' case, the sign was profound—a divine voice thundering at his baptism. Today the indications of election are likely to be bodied forth more subtly, via an illuminating remark, a life-changing service, an enduring glow of kindness or wisdom that draws others irresistibly to the possessor. Nevertheless, such signs will be there for the seeing, reassuring us that incarnate holiness still lives among us, in humble, unexpected contexts as well as in splashy, well-publicized ones.

Be it ever so humble, no community goes unblessed by God.

Meditation: If you meet with others regularly for prayer, Bible study, or fellowship, dedicate a meeting to sharing appreciative stories of the holiness in your community. Each group member should be on the lookout for someone who carries a special spark of God, made manifest in some specific way. Celebrate these extraordinary individuals—and your extraordinary community—with thanksgiving.

Prayer: God of the humble, let me never doubt your ability to work in any setting, any person—including mine and me.

Real Presence

Readings: 1 John 5:5-13; Mark 1:7-11 or Luke 3:23-38 or
3:23, 31-34, 36, 38

Scripture:
This is the one who came through water and Blood, Jesus
Christ . . . God gave us eternal life, and this life is in his Son.
(1 John 5:5, 11)

Reflection: "I feel like I've spent *so* much time in church over
Advent and Christmas! And wasn't it tempting this morning,
with the snow falling and the dark, to sleep in? But here we
are—always the good Catholic girls, I guess." My friend
smiles ruefully as she greets me after Mass.

I smile back, remembering how warm my own bed felt,
and on the careful drive home I take pleasure in imagining
all the saints ensconced in that unimaginably warm and
lovely heaven who might be nodding in approval of us
"good Catholic girls" right now. I think about a passage in
today's Gospel that rang with deep relevance to a dilemma
I'm facing, and hug to my heart the joy I felt during a favorite
hymn.

I remember the periods in my life when I didn't go to
church regularly, feeling like God had abandoned me (or at
least was ignoring me). I pitifully imagined I was delivering
a tit for tat. Not just my spiritual but my psychological being

suffered in those intervals when I cut myself off from the grace of community and sacrament, and the eventual home-comings were manna.

There's attendance and there's *attendance*, of course, as I admittedly still need to remind myself. It's one thing to show up grudgingly, obsessed by pending chores or enjoyments, barely listening. It's another to really take in the homily and reflect on the Scriptures, to feel faith swell when sparked by the transcendental beauty of a shaft of light through stained glass, or by another's face lit with joy or yearning.

The term "holy day of obligation" might seem to suggest we come to Mass from enforced duty to a God who needs our attention for his good. In fact, we're called to attend for our own.

Meditation: Recall personally important, uplifting moments you've experienced at Mass. Did help for a specific problem come? What triggered insight or comfort? Did you allow that inspiration to influence the following hours/days/weeks? Vow to look for such a moment at every Mass, actively cultivating its fruit.

Prayer: Loving Christ, open my spirit to apprehend the "mountaintop" moments that public worship offers. Ever-renew my hunger for the sacraments.

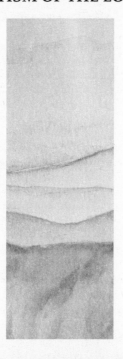

EPIPHANY AND
BAPTISM OF THE LORD

True Wisdom

Readings: Isa 60:1-6; Eph 3:2-3a, 5-6; Matt 2:1-12

Scripture:
O God, with your judgment endow the king,
   and with your justice, the king's son. (Ps 72:1)

Reflection: After a lifetime of working in a university setting, I've come to wish that more academics—and others who aspire to wisdom, including our political leaders—were more like the magi. Too often today's "wise ones" spend their time investigating ever-more-narrowly-specialized fields, defending pet theories. They decry ways of knowing not their own, seeking niched prestige and patronage. The magi, in contrast, drew the priestly advice they offered kings from a variety of disciplines, including mathematics, astronomy, history, alchemy, and astrology.

That combination of broad, deep study and reverent openness to the "beyond" was essential in inspiring the epiphany we celebrate today. Charting the heavens and earth led the magi to the baby Jesus; openness to plumbing a dream's divinely inspired message helped thwart Herod's deadly scheme.

There's nothing wrong with expert command of a field, of course. Yet when we base our judgments solely on a narrow, purely scientific perspective, we betray that multifaceted, eons-old human heritage of deeper knowing so crucial in the magi's story.

On this day when we celebrate those venerable followers of the "star of wonder," may we rededicate ourselves to looking not just down at our books, but up at the heavens too.

Meditation: In our highly specialized culture, decision-making is often based on one source or the perspective of one set of experts. The next time you need to decide something, borrow the magi's spirit and seek information from multiple sources, multiple disciplines. Avoid rushing to judgment and allow yourself time and space for the Holy Spirit's guidance.

Prayer: God of Wisdom, when I must make a judgment in my personal, professional, or spiritual life, give me the courage to investigate widely and the confidence to listen for your voice.

The Ever-Renewing Consecration

Readings: Isa 42:1-4, 6-7 or Acts 10:34-38; Mark 1:7-11

Scripture:
Give to the LORD, you sons of God,
   give to the LORD glory and praise. (Ps 29:1)

Reflection: "Why does the sinless Jesus need to be baptized?" people ask in religious education classes. "Isn't baptism a sacrament that washes away sin?"

Well, yes, it is. But, as theologians tell us, Jesus' baptism added a new dimension to such washing-away. The ceremonial cleansing practiced by his Jewish contemporaries was a repeatable ritual; Jesus' baptism is a dramatic one-time anointing that publicly marks his sacred calling. It's also a precedent, as St. Maximus explained, that gives new identity to his followers: "When the Savior is washed, all water for our baptism is made clean, purified at its source for the dispensing of baptismal grace to the people of future ages. . . . He wants you to become a living force for all . . . , lights shining in the world."

Baptism, then, is the formal beginning of our lives as people dedicated to God's service, as "lights shining." What daunting responsibilities, what joys and glories that state promises! Death's terror vanishes, since as people "baptized into [Christ's] death" along with his ministry, we're bound to accept his resurrection (Rom 6:3-4). We're free to live with attentive peace, to ask in absolute trust, "What do you want of me, Lord? How do you want me to serve you?"

Thus, for all who happily count themselves among the baptized, Ordinary Time—dawning at the end of this very day—should never be just "ordinary." The Advent and Christmas seasons might be over for the year, but our festive celebration of Christ's presence, our sharing of blessings with each other, will continue through all the days ahead.

O come, let us adore him.

Meditation: If today were the day of your baptism, what intentions would you be nurturing for the year ahead? To which aspects of Christian life, what forms of service would you choose to be dedicated? What shape would your adoration take? Let the answers guide your path as Ordinary Time unfolds.

Prayer: Ever-faithful God, may the blessings of these sacred seasons of Advent and Christmas linger in my soul and guide me on the road ahead.

References

Introduction
Pope Francis, Address for the Feast of the Immaculate Conception, December 8, 2020.

December 3: First Sunday of Advent
St. Teresa of Avila, *Exclamations of the Soul to God*, 15:3. Included in *Catechism of the Catholic Church*, 2nd ed. (United States Catholic Conference—Libreria Editrice Vaticana, 1997), 1821.

December 8:
The Immaculate Conception of the Blessed Virgin Mary
John Henry Newman, *God's Will the End of Life: Discourses Addressed to Mixed Congregations* (Aeterna Press, 2015).

December 11: Monday of the Second Week of Advent
C. S. Lewis, "Miracles," in *God in the Dock: Essays on Theology and Ethics*, ed. Walter Hooper (Grand Rapids, MI: Eerdmans, 1970).

December 15: Friday of the Second Week of Advent
Pope Francis, *Evangelii Gaudium*, The Joy of the Gospel (Vatican City: Libreria Editrice Vaticana, 2013), 1.

December 17: Third Sunday of Advent
St. Thomas Aquinas, *Summa Theologica*, Question 28.
Joni Mitchell, "Court and Spark," from *Court and Spark*, 1974.

December 27: Saint John the Apostle
For books on death, see:

Joan Chittister, *The Gift of Years: Growing Older Gracefully* (New York: BlueBridge, 2008).

Richard Rohr, *Falling Upward: A Spirituality for the Two Halves of Life* (San Francisco: Jossey-Bass, 2011).

Susan Swetnam, *In the Mystery's Shadow: Reflections on Caring for the Elderly and Dying* (Collegeville, MN: Liturgical Press, 2019).

January 3: Wednesday, Christmas Weekday
For a look at early Christian expressions of this theme, see Bart

Ehrmann, *Journeys to Heaven and Hell: Tours of the Afterlife in the Early Christian Tradition* (New Haven: Yale University Press, 2022).

"In the Sweet By and By," lyrics by S. Fillmore Bennett, music by Joseph P. Webster, 1868.

January 8: The Baptism of the Lord

Sermons of St. Maximus of Turin, trans. Boniface Ramsey, OP, Ancient Christian Writers Series (Mahwah, NJ: Paulist Press, 1989), #100.